MAKING 100 MILLION DOLLARS FROM NFT

How To Design And Upload 10,000 Nfts For Free

John Welsh

MAKING 100 MILLION DOLLARS FROM NFT

At the risk of sounding like a broken record, we do need to point out that all of the content in this book is purely for informational purposes. None of it is financial advice. NFTs are an extremely new asset class. If you thought cryptocurrency was risky, please be aware that NFTs are even riskier. Please make sure that you have done your own research before investing and never invest more than you are willing to lose. The vast majority of people will lose money in this market.

First Edition: Mar 2022

10 9 8 7 6 5 4 3 2 1

NFT: A NEW WAY OF MAKING MONEY FROM CRYPTOCURRENCY

Over the past few years, NFTs have slowly crept into the public lexicon. Nowadays, everywhere you look you see articles about big-ticket NFT sales.

A significant turning point for the scene hit in 2018, when artist Kevin Abosch partnered with GIFTO for a charitable auction with NFTs placed at the forefront. The partnership resulted in a $1M sale of a piece named Forever Rose.

Since then, the market has soared higher and higher. In 2021, Beeple broke the internet, when he sold a piece for $69 million, officially making NFTs a household name.

The most popular question asked is "How do you make money from NFT?"

This is a very important question and it should be attended to in a well-elaborated manner.

In this book, I explained everything you need to make money from NFT. Starting from the creating and minting your first NFT.

This is a practical book and you need to be ready to take actions to fully benefit from this book.

A GLANCE INTO THE BOOK

TABLE OF CONTENTS

A Million Dollar JPEG

If you're just getting into the NFT scene, you're probably wondering what the answer is. Why are people spending so much money on NFTs if they're just a JPEG image that you could easily save or screenshot? Further to that, why are so many vocal skeptics questioning their value? To answer this question, we first need to understand the Technology Adoption Cycle.

Many people have heard about NFTs, but only the early adopters have started to use the technology - the rest are grappling with understanding its practical applications.

The general public's understanding of why digital art is valuable if they could simply "take a screenshot" brings a core value proposition of NFT technology into question; its ability to prove ownership.

Provenance of The Art World

The value of NFT technology becomes easier to understand when we take a step back to examine how art dealing operates in the real world.

Firstly, the art world is full of forgery. Though it is becoming more challenging, fake Picassos, Rothcos, and Monets slip through the cracks and sell for millions at auctions from time to time. Auction houses do their best to combat fraud. The first port of call is to examine the provenance of the piece.

Provenance is a form of documentation that commonly accompanies art pieces. It details the ownership history of a piece. If the verifier is lucky, the list will trace right back to the original artist. Once a believable ownership history has been established, the examiner will proceed to test the artwork using a laundry list of methods - from examining the makeup of paint pigments to compare it with the paints commonly used at the time, to testing the age of canvas fibers. Many testing mechanisms are used because it is easy to fake any single one (even provenance) but challenging to get all of them right.

Verifying an artwork is a long and expensive process - so why is it done? The answer seems obvious - because art buyers want to know they're getting the real deal. A copy, no matter how perfect, is not enough. Buyers pay for more than just the artwork - they're paying for a spot in the chain of ownership of the piece - its provenance. Provenance is what makes owning an original Picasso (and not just a print from a museum gift shop) so special.

Digital Provenance

At their core, NFT technology enables trackable, transparent ownership. Each time an NFT is transferred to someone else, it is recorded on the blockchain - for all to see.

From the moment an NFT is created on the blockchain, future owners of that NFT will have a provable chain of ownership leading right back to the Creator.

Digital Provenance was never possible before NFTs came onto the digital art scene and is precisely why the art world is going crazy for it. NFT technology gives a file (in this case, a JPEG) an irrefutable ownership history - something that even real-world provenance documents cannot do.

Further to that, because NFTs aren't fungible (are unique and cannot be replaced), the buyer has proof that they are the sole owner of an art piece, issued by the artist. That means that NFT technology could place digital artworks in the same spot of cultural significance as real-world art: many people can see and enjoy them, and they can even get ahold of free copies of them, but we know that an individual owns the original copy linked to the artist.

The Art World Was Amazed By The Technology

"Non-fungible" more or less means that it's unique and can't be replaced with something else. For example, a bitcoin is fungible — trade one for another bitcoin, and you'll have exactly the same thing. A one-of-a-kind trading card, however, is non-fungible. If you traded it for a different card, you'd have something completely different.

They are built on blockchains. These distributed public ledgers record transactions. Each NFT is stored on the blockchain with an identification code and metadata that makes it as unique as a fingerprint. In this context, "metadata" means "data about data" and is simply a bit of extra information that describes the NFT and is stored alongside it.

They're an excellent way to mark digital assets and control their supply. Whether you've created a piece of music, a digital artwork or video, "minting" it as an NFT means that you can prove ownership over it (as each NFT is distinct and traceable). Previously, digital assets were fairly easy to steal. This is huge as it means artists can't be cheated out of royalties anymore and collectors don't have to worry about investing in something that's a fake or a forgery.

This is also an excellent way to control supply of digital content, which is key to driving up its price. Because it attributes one owner to one piece of content, even if others can see the NFT, only one person can own it.

Think of them as digital receipts or signatures. If you're a collector, NFTs can be considered the digital equivalent of the kind of receipt you'd get after you've bought something physical (like clothing or food) from your favorite store. As an artist, turning your work into an NFT is a way of adding a digital signature that can never be forged or removed.

So whether you're able to purchase limited first edition prints for large sums or starting up your collection with a piece that costs $1, working with NFTs makes sure that everybody wins. The artist is credited for their work (and are paid royalties in perpetuity), you're credited as the rightful owner, and nobody is being priced out of the market by (or losing money to) elitist intermediaries.

Creators' NFT table

When an artist chooses to mint their work and turn it into an NFT, they turn it into a digital collector's item.

So whether you're minting a one-of-a-kind piece of content or sharing a limited edition of 25 prints, you're able to create digital scarcity — allowing your work to gain in value. So, if you've minted a digital artwork, someone who has a copy of it they've pulled from a Google Image search may enjoy it privately but they won't be able to sell it and cut you out of the royalty chain (or claim the work as their own). Unless their copy is an NFT, it's immediately identifiable as a fake — NFTs can only have one owner at a time, and each one is unique.

Can NFTs be copied, stolen or hacked? Copied? No. Hacked? Unfortunately, yes they can. But that's only if your NFT platform suffers from slack cybersecurity measures or user accounts aren't properly protected with strong passwords.

Why NFTs Are Here To Stay

NFTs are all the buzz at the moment. Every artist seems to be talking about them. You've probably heard about young artists making millions from selling their digital works, or how In just the first three months of 2021, more than $2 billion worth of NFTs were sold

But what does it mean for you an artist? Well, creating an NFT of your work enables you to prove digital ownership, create scarcity of your work, and earn money from your work.

If you're looking to get into creating and selling NFTs, you've come to the right place. From finding the perfect platform to create and showcase your work, to helping you avoid the most common pitfalls, we've got you covered. We'll even share some tips on how to generate marketing buzz around your work!

Lets dive in at the start - creating (known as Minting) your first NFT.

What it means to mint an NFT and why it benefits creators

When you transform your digital work — image, music, video or otherwise — you store it as data on a blockchain, a distributed public ledger. This process is called "minting"

While this may not automatically protect your work under copyright, it's an excellent way to mark the digital assets you're creating, and control their supply. By turning your digital art into a scarce object — no longer easily duplicated — it protects the value of your work and ensures you get paid a fair price and recognised as the rightful author.

The top three pitfalls of minting NFTs, and how to avoid them

Here are the three most common pitfalls you may encounter when you're starting out in the NFT market:

1. Hidden gas fees, or fake 'free' minting.

Minting an NFT takes energy, in the form of computing power. "Gas fees" are the payments users of an NFT-platform make to compensate for the cost of the computing power used to process and validate this transaction on the blockchain.

Sometimes, platforms claim to offer free minting (no payment of gas fees required) but neglect to highlight this offer is only valid under certain circumstances — like if your artwork is paid for in cryptocurrency instead of USD, or if you only accept offers that match or exceed your asking price.

For example, let's compare the fee structures of five established NFT platforms:

OpenSea. Dubbed "the ebay of NFT marketplaces", they're a marketplace that curates and sells art from other platforms while allowing users to mint NFTs directly on OpenSea. They don't charge an upfront gas fee (due to their use of a process known as "lazy minting") but grab a 2.5% marketplace fee for each sale. Further to that fee, you have to pay gas fees upon accepting an offer to purchase your NFT. These gas fees can be anywhere between $50-$800 or more depending on how busy the network is.

SuperRare. Artists on this exclusive platform are charged a 3% fee and 15% marketplace fee for every sale.

Mintable. Another playform that uses 'lazy minting', Mintable, doesn't charge an upfront fee. Instead, users pay transaction fees based on what they're selling: 2.5% on normal items; 5% for gasless items and 10% on printable series.

Momint. A free minting NFT marketplace. They charge a 15% commission on sales.

2. NFT fraud and Sleep minting

For now, you technically don't need to own the copyright to mint something. This can leave unsuspecting artists unprotected, as the NFT-community learned when some unscrupulous characters took "proof of concept" a step too far when minting and selling work they didn't create. There have also been structural flaws in SMART CONTRACTS which have left unprotected NFTs open to reproduction — minting extra editions without the artist being aware of it.

Some NFT platforms' have different approach to security, copyright and authenticity:

Opensea. To qualify for account verification, you must have at least 10,000 followers on Twitter or Instagram. Artists with smaller followings are therefore left wide-open to the risk of impersonation — as the OpenSea team won't consider reviewing (and hopefully, verifying) smaller accounts. Unfortunately, an artist's social media popularity isn't a reliable judge of their skill, and Twitter and Instagrams' identity verification methods aren't known for being thorough!

Rarible. To be verified as an artist on Rarible, your account is manually reviewed by a staff member. However, as the Laufman saga proved, this is open to error — all someone has to do is have a completed profile, with at least one minted item!

SuperRare. Artists hoping to sell their work on SuperRare have to pass a fairly strict application process, which includes proving their identity. In addition to the fairly standard requirement of linking to social media sites or online portfolios, artists also have to provide a short video explaining the story behind your art. Competition for space on this platform is fierce, however, and it can put digital creators who are just starting out (or who don't have teams of their own marketing assistants) at a significant disadvantage.

3. Minter's regret

Activity on the blockchain is indelible; 3the permanence of each transaction is kind of the point. But that means that there's no room for error, as once you've minted a piece, you've minted it for life.

Minting NFTs: Winning tips to boost your success

Let's switch the focus to how you can boost your chances of success as an NFT artist. We've distilled it down to four important tips:

1. Learn from other NFT artists

Start following established artists you enjoy, and dive into the NFT community on the social media platform of your choice. This quick way to glean tips and tricks can boost your artistic skill and crypto-savvy.

2. Tell the story behind your work

It's proven that you're much more likely to remember something, if you know the story behind it. Through storytelling, you're also able to develop a deeper connection between yourself and your audience.

Think of the nature of NFTs themselves: someone will take pride in their ability to own it forever. Embrace this significance and sentimentality and tell the story of how you came to be a digital creator, and the inspiration behind your work.

3. Engage with, and grow, your community

When someone collects your work, it's always good to acknowledge them and say thank you. Engage with collectors and creators on Twitter, Discord and other social media platforms to gain exposure within the community.

In these ways, you can establish personal connections with those who appreciate your work and network with others in the community.

4. Give your audience context

The NFT industry is only just beginning and, as an early adopter, it's important to give audiences who aren't familiar with NFTs some context. Let them know why you're creating them. Introducing your friends, family and fellow artists to the NFT space can help sell your work and grow your community faster than you would otherwise expect.

CHARACTERISTICS OF A GOOD NFT

PROJECT

Uniqueness plays a large role in the overall value of NFT projects, including in the utility that can be offered through an NFT's traits. Creating a proper unique strategy can add to the excitement of an NFT project's collectors.

Creating an excellent unique strategy for your NFT project is a crucial step in executing a successful NFT launch, as well as sustaining your NFT project long-term. A good unique strategy helps collectors find what they are looking for easily and ensures your NFT project is exciting.

Quantity

The more art you provide the more the value. Do not get me wrong, the price of some single NFTs are much more than the price of some group NFTs.

Nevertheless, quantity gives you more possibilities of sales. I may like a different flavor of candy other than the flavor you like. This is the reason why you need to create many varieties for your NFT project.

Moreover, a lot of NFT meters uses the varieties an NFT has to judge if an NFT project is worth investing in or not. Though, this is not a reliable yardstick, but it show commitment and effort.

Quality

Before you can determine what traits your NFT project will have, first you need to create the traits categories. The main purpose of traits categories is to help organize all the unique traits.

Some examples of trait categories can be a jacket, hat, facial expression, and what the character is holding in their mouth. Each category would then have a certain number of unique traits, which are more specific, and each unique trait would appear a certain number of times in the NFT collection.

Rarity Sniper recommends having a minimum of seven trait categories in your NFT project to keep your collection visually exciting

1. Unique traits

You can't develop a proper rarity strategy without creating individual traits. As mentioned in the previous section, traits go under your trait categories. For instance, with the example of the trait category of a jacket, your unique traits might be "gold jacket," "blue jacket," "leather jacket," etc.

You can then choose how often each individual trait appears in your collection. For instance, a gold jacket might appear five times and a blue jacket 505 times.

Individual traits are an essential part of any rarity strategy and are the foundation for many NFT projects. When creating traits for your NFTs, you want to make sure that you have at least 150 traits.

The more traits you have, the more diverse your project will be. However, if you make too many traits, a project can quickly become overwhelming.

Likewise, if you fail to create enough traits, your project can appear undiversified and remain stagnant.

2. Rare traits

Within your set of unique traits, you should strive to include rare traits. These rare traits should not exceed more than 1 percent of your NFT project's total quantity. If your project has 1,000 NFTs, then only ten of those NFTs should have rare traits.

For example, in the popular Bored Ape Yacht Club collection, the "Laser Eyes" trait appears in less than 1 percent of NFTs. The fact that it appears so few times in the collection makes it an ultra-rare trait.

Rare traits can add additional value to your NFT project by creating scarcity within the collection. This means that NFTs with rare traits might be more valuable than those with common traits. Rare traits add to the excitement of collectors.

3. Low visual impact traits

When creating your NFT's unique traits, avoid traits that don't have a significant impact on the visual aspect of your NFTs such as earrings or other small objects.

An example of a low visual impact trait to avoid comes, again, from the Bored Ape Yacht collection. The trait category in question is the "earring." The "gold stud earring" is very small to the point where you can barely see it.

Avoid the use of low visual impact traits that will prevent your NFT project from looking diverse and exciting. If you use a less noticeable unique trait, your NFTs may all look the same and as a result, may appear unappealing to potential collectors.

4. One-of-one and legendary traits

The next level of rarity that you should include in your NFT project is one-of-one and legendary traits. These extremely limited-edition traits can provide your project and collectors with added value and excitement.

An example of one-to-one traits is in the Cool Cats collection. There are several Cool Cats that are drawn one-of-one, meaning they don't have any generative art traits. In part, because they are so rare, they're very valuable.

You want to avoid having too many legendary traits though, as this can result in the top of the rankings for your NFT project to all rank number one. Rarity Sniper says that the optimal number of legendary trait NFTs they see in projects are limited to ten NFTs in the entire collection.

5. Media used

The last thing that you should consider when creating an excellent rarity strategy for your NFT project is the type of media used. Media refers to the asset used to create the NFT. You can choose to use images, animation, video, and audio to spruce up your NFT project.

Rarity Sniper recommends using a mix of media to diversify your NFT project and help differentiate the levels of rarities.

For example, you can have your more common rarities as static images and then make legendary NFTs animated. This tactic separates the legendary NFTs from the common NFTs, as seen in the Boryoku Dragonz NFT collection.

Collectors can then quickly distinguish the more desirable NFTs in a project. Differentiating media helps keep the project exciting and capture the imagination of anyone who may be viewing it.

Another way to implement unique media is to collaborate with influencers and other artists in the space. You can have an artist design traits for your project, or you can even incorporate an influencer to be represented as one of the NFTs in your project.

Good Story Line

Now, to be quite frank, you should always take these roadmaps with a grain of salt. As GaryVee has said on multiple occasions, roadmaps are nothing but a startup's pitch deck.

And a pitch deck is never a guarantee that something will actually happen, they are merely a promise at a point in time that a founding team plans to do something.

So if someone asks what makes a good NFT project, the roadmap shouldn't be your first response.

Remember, you are buying into a vision and the likelihood of that materializing will largely depend on the ability of the founders to actually execute it. The vast majority of startups fail and the same holds true for NFT projects.

That being said, a roadmap will give you an indication of what the end goal of the project is and that will help you decide whether the project is for you or not. We have an excellent article on NFT roadmap examples that we recommend you have a look at too.

If you do not believe in "play-to-earn" games, then you probably shouldn't invest in a project that plans to create such a game. If you'd like to find out more about the best NFT games right now, we have an excellent article on the subject.

An NFT Roadmap is a document that maps out the goals and strategies of an NFT project you are currently looking into, in order to communicate its long-term value. NFT roadmaps usually include key project milestones, short and long-term goals, and plans for marketing and growth. It is the same as with regular businesses. It needs a clear vision and mission. We need to look at how it is built up and how much effort was given to putting the pieces together. Is what they want to achieve even feasible? Follow your gut... if it seems like it does not make sense, then it probably won't.

Website And Social Media

Not every NFT project needs a community, but a vibrant community is a strong indicator of a promising project. If you ask Twitter, what makes a good NFT project, the vast majority will probably refer to the community.

A big community of followers is not only an effective tool in marketing a project, it can also become a core value proposition. Holders of an NFT of a project are financially invested and their incentives are aligned with those of the team.

Being part of a community with exclusive access privileges also helps build brand loyalty because people want to remain part of an exclusive "club". Positive and inclusive communities tend to perform well because they are fun to hang out in and they foster a culture of reciprocal promotion. We highly recommend that you spend at least a few hours inside a project's Discord server in order to assess not only how active the community is but also how responsive the founding team is.

PR is a hugely underestimated marketing tool.

If a project makes the headlines of big media outlets, the additional exposure for that project will almost certainly increase its likelihood of success. Just like you are reading this article right now, trying to figure out what makes a good NFT project, most people tend to gravitate towards the things that have been mentioned in the media.

This makes sense because media exposure helps build brand recognition and if the project vision is to become a streetwear brand, then brand building to by far the most crucial part of the endeavor. This also includes celebrities who have picked up their own NFTs of the project.

Exposure via the social media channels of well-known celebrities is very likely to boost the perception of that project. Social proof is a powerful thing in social media.

Create A Good Trustworthy Team

Does the founding team have experience in running a project like this?

What skills do the founders bring to the table and are they the necessary skills to pull off a successful NFT project?

Do they even know what makes a good NFT project?

Some of the key skills that a project needs include social media marketing, brand management, community management/PR, blockchain development and ideally an artist with a signature style. It might seem counterintuitive that the art is non-essential but it's true.

Bear in mind, we're not talking about die-hard artists who live for their work and are aspiring to move up the ranks of the most expensive NFTs ever sold.

Artistic merit is subjective and some very successful projects have objectively horrible artwork. The question isn't what makes good NFT art, but what ingredients make a successful project. Bored Ape Yacht Club, currently the most successful project to have ever existed, had all its artwork done by a freelancer for a one-time fee.

Once a project is successful and has an established style, it's relatively easy for other talented artists to imitate it and thereby fill the gaps.

Ideally, you'd also want the team to be fully doxxed, meaning that their identities are public. It's easier for anonymous teams to abandon a project if their personal reputations are not on the line. Doxxed teams are more likely to pull through in the long run.

It is important that the project discloses information about the participants as much as possible. It's cool when the profiles of the founders are stylized as the characters of the project:

Expertise of team members is an extremely important aspect. If the artists of the project have worked on well-known projects of companies such as Pixar, Dreamworks, and have weight in the art community, all this is an absolute plus. The experience of the team participating in other Crypto projects - projects - will also be a plus. I will also include partnerships with other cool teams and projects

A plus will be the maintenance of social networks by team members using project content

Relevance And Value

A lot of the early NFT projects primarily focused on the artistic aspect. And that still holds true if the primary objective of the project is to create or promote some form of art (e.g. digital art, music, film, etc).

For many people, this isn't enough though and NFTs enable a whole new category of investments which the world has seen before, however not necessarily in this form.

"Utility" is becoming an increasingly important aspect of many project's roadmaps.

So what makes a good NFT project? Is it utility?

With increasing NFT prices many late investors obviously want to know how the team plans to bring additional value to its holders which will help increase the token's price.

There are roughly 2 different categories of utility that have emerged.

The first category involves some form of real-life utility, such as access to a conference, exclusive access to a high-end restaurant chain or in its simplest form, access to merchandise.

The second category is purely digital in nature and can involve access to certain areas within the project's Discord, early access to content, access to play-to-earn blockchain games or even yield from the project's own ecosystem token. That's right, some projects actually provide a form of yield.

Gamefication & Game Theory

You may want to invest in a project for its real-life utility or the social credit that it gives you in public. However, the vast majority of people are primarily looking to make a profit.

Some projects have developed complex ecosystems where certain tokens or combinations of multiple tokens may have more value than others because they yield a different type of token. And these tokens are required in order to pay for things within the ecosystem.

Most of the mechanisms are designed to incentive holding tokens for as long as possible and not list them on marketplaces. Less listed tokens mean that supply is limited and with growing demand, the price of the tokens will go up as well.

This is also where the total number of unique token holders comes into play. A project with a very high ratio of unique holders will be inherently more stable in price because if everyone only has 1 token, they are less likely to sell it.

So is this what makes a good NFT project?

Price Stability & Endurance

As mentioned in the last section, a high holder count will usually result in more stable prices.

A project with a history of stable growth and only limited hype-driven swings is usually a better investment because they are an indicator of long-term holders.

A good example of such a project is Veefriends by GaryVee. Big swings driven by hype are usually a sign of a lot of day traders, who feed off of the pumps and subsequent dumps in order to make a profit.

They are rarely interested in the long-term viability of a project. Price history also comes into play when a project has already been around for a while. Was there a single huge pump at the time of mint and then it just fizzled out over time?

Or did the price actually recover over time because the team kept building?

You can keep track of the NFT prices in your portfolio by using one of many NFT tracking tools. In this asset class, the survivors are the winners.

No one knows what projects will come out on top, so your primary objective should be to pick the survivors. That's why so many people are asking what makes a good NFT?

BEST NFTS TO CREATE NOW

As an NFT designer or creator, There some generally global unique concepts that you should consider looking into. One of these concepts is Monkey Pirates. This concept can make you a millionaire. Listed below are other good unique project and concepts I think you can work on right now.

Gangster Rabbit: Not A regular looking rabbit with gangster concept. This NFT concept will be a muscular Rabbit, torn clothes, gangster hairstyle or cap, tattooed, and must have marks of injuries sustained from cuts and gun wounds. Some of the NFTs may include smoking, Firearms, and drugs.

Samurai Rat: Just like the master rat in ninja turtle, this rat would be a typical Samurai with a stylish rat concept. This NFT would include the normal Samurai costume, cute looking rate with regular body.

Kunfu Panda Pro: There are many concept you can create with the Kunfu Panda character. Just be creative and think uniquely.

Meditation Sounds Pack: An NFT can be a media file, therefore, you can as well create Sounds and videos. A meditation sound pack is the great Idea. You can decide to

Video Memes Pack: Memes are a way social media interacts these days. Most meme creators don't get credit for their fabulous work. You can change that. Creating Meme NFT is a very good idea.

Workout Tiger: This is another JPEG NFT project concept. Most workout animations are usually a Tiger, Bull, or Bear. A Tiger workout NFT would include different workout concepts using a Tiger as case study. You have to be creative with this one.

Angry Kingkong Pro: Kong is always pictured angry. This is also a good concept any NFT designer should capitalize on. Making an Angry KingKong will take a little more work because you wouldn't want to make look like the original KIngKong.

HOW TO MINT YOUR NFT ON OPENSEA

FOR FREE

The most crucial part of an NFT project is to mint it to an interested market. Over the years, many NFT projects have been launched and sold successfully on NFT markets like OpenSea.

At the same time, hundreds of NFT projects are still on their way to make it to the market. Most times, this is because of lack of funds to launch and mint it to the market.

Independent NFT creator or designer lack sponsorship to market their NFT project.

Most Dominant Network On OpenSea:

The most popular network on OpenSea is the Ethereum network. This is the network where most NFT project are on. The popularity of the Ethereum on OpenSea is as a result of the popularity of the Ethereum Blockchain and the Ethereum coin. Therefore, it is advisable that a designer mint his project on the network for two reasons; 1. The popularity of the Ethereum network, And 2. Because most Investors and Buyers are more familiar with the network than any other networks.

There is a disadvantage though, minting your NFT is not free and requires some fees to get started.

The Free Networks:

Do not be discouraged yet. You can still mint your NFT on OpenSea without paying any fees or charges. However, you can only do that through the polygon network. In the following steps, I will explain how to do this in less than 5 minutes.

Create A Metamask Wallet: First you need a Metamask wallet created preferably on your smartphone. Therefore, download the Metamask App, register for a free account, and save your seed phrase somewhere safe. You will be given a free wallet on Ethereum main network.

Create A Polygon Network Wallet: Open MetaMask and click the network dropdown menu.

Now, click [Add Network] on the pop-up.

You'll need to add the following details on the [Add a network] page that will open. Click [Save] when you're finished.

Page | 30

Network Name	Polygon
New RPC URL	Choose any of the following: https://polygon-rpc.com https://rpc-mainnet.maticvigil.com https://rpc-mainnet.matic.network https://rpc-mainnet.matic.quiknode.pro
Chain ID	137
Currency Symbol	MATIC
Block Explorer URL	https://polygonscan.com/

Networks > Add a network

A malicious network provider can lie about the state of the blockchain and record your network activity. Only add custom networks you trust.

Network Name

Polygon

New RPC URL

https://polygon-rpc.com

Chain ID ⓘ

137

Currency Symbol (Optional)

MATIC

Block Explorer URL (Optional)

https://polygonscan.com/

Cancel   Save

Add To Opensea: After the above exercise, go to opensea.io and create a free account. Link your polygon metamask wallet to the account. This would allow you to upload your NFT without having to pay any fee.

Mint Nft For Free: Upload your readymade NFT project to OpenSea.

INVESTING IN AN NFT PROJECT

From an investing perspective, buying an NFT is even riskier than buying crypto because it is almost like a leveraged bet on crypto. It is essentially gambling but people don't really know the difference and they buy them because they're fun.

On the other hand, a lot of people are buying NFTs not as investments but simply because they are fun or bring them joy. Crypto expert Laura Shin is one of them. She purchased an NFT related to music, but she says her decision was driven by emotion, not investment.

NFTs are not quite ready for primetime investing, and there are several aspects of crypto you'll want to be really comfortable with before you find yourself owning an NFT.

For one, the process to buy an NFT is complicated. You need an Ethereum-compatible crypto wallet and some ether to get started, and you have to connect your wallet to an NFT marketplace — a lot of hoops to jump through. NFTs are also susceptible to crypto hacks and scams, which have become increasingly common and sophisticated. A Google search for "NFT scams" shows just how much opportunity there is to run into trouble.

And then there's the question of value and utility. NFTs are not like a stock or a bond where you generally know the intrinsic value of that investment. A successful NFT is similar to a strong brand, and a lot of value is given to it by other people, so it's only as valuable as someone else is willing to pay for it.

For the average investor, it's generally a bad idea unless you just want to buy into it for the artwork, and you're OK with never seeing that money again. There's so much inherent risk in NFTs.

Knowing that NFTs are risky, speculative assets like crypto, you'll need to determine your level of exposure to them. Generally, experts say most long-term investors will be better served by allocating only a small portion of their portfolio (less than 5%, and never at the expense of meeting other financial goals) to cryptocurrency rather than to an NFT.

Investors' Table

NFTs have exploded in popularity during the pandemic, leading many investors to wonder how to buy them.

Artists, collectors, and speculators alike have flocked to the movement as cryptocurrencies and other digital assets have skyrocketed in price. The jury's still out on whether this is an unsustainable bubble ready to pop, or if this is the birth of a new long-term investment asset class.

Not sure what NFTs are and how to get started investing in them -- or whether you should in the first place? Here's what you need to know.

How To Buy NFTs

NFTs are bought and sold via a purpose-built NFT marketplace, kind of like Amazon or Etsy, only for digital assets. These marketplaces can be used to buy an NFT at a fixed price or function as a virtual auction, much like the exchange system for buying and selling cryptocurrencies and stocks. Prices on NFTs listed for sale via auction are therefore volatile, changing in value depending on demand. The higher the demand, the higher the price.

There are a variety of marketplaces that support NFT purchases.

To invest in NFTs, you need to open and fund the correct crypto wallet. Then, you can place a bid on your desired NFT.

Identifying And Selecting Profitable NFT

The NFT movement is new and is an early demonstration of the potential cryptos have to make the digital economy work for more people. Creating and selling digital assets might make a lot of sense for creators. But when it comes to buying NFTs for their value as a collectible, they are a speculative investment. Value is uncertain and will fluctuate based on demand for the work itself.

There's no set rule for figuring out which collectible will increase in value and which one won't. But identifying a new NFT trend early can pay off big later on. Some digital works of art that originally sold for petty values have gone on to sell for many thousands of dollars.

If you have an eye for art, music, etc., and you enjoy collecting, dabbling in NFT investing might make sense for you. Some things to look for when buying include the creator of the asset, how unique the piece is, the history of the asset's ownership, and whether, once owned, an asset could be used to generate income (for example, payment to view a piece or relicensing fees).

As to the argument that NFTs are a "bubble" waiting to pop, bubbles are usually only revealed in hindsight. But bear in mind that doesn't change the fact that digital assets could indeed cool off at some point in the future. Weigh the risks, and diversify your investments -- perhaps by mixing in cryptos as well as stocks of businesses developing blockchain technology to your NFT portfolio.

NFTs are in the early days of development. It's a promising new front in the world of technology, but risks abound when investing in any movement's nascent stage. Tread lightly as you learn more about NFTs, and remember to stay diversified with your investments to limit the risk of any single asset derailing your wealth-building progress.

When To Sell Your NFT

Most NFTs represent static assets that don't generate any income on their own, they are primarily valued by subjective metrics such as buyer demand.

But if you have eye for good Arts, Music and Viral Videos you will end up selling your NFT faster than you expected. You must also have good marketing skill for your NFT to yield better profit.

The decision of selling is totally up to you. You have to make up your mind to sell your NFT when you deem it right. But there are some conditions you need to consider in order to get good RIO from your NFT.

The following will help you sell your NFT for a better price:

1. Placing a bid on your NFT could help you sell it fast.

2. When you see a decent offer for your NFT, sell it. You must not be greedy.

3. If there is any offer for any of your NFT that is little or more above your buying price, you can sell.

4. If a similar NFT goes Viral, you may consider selling yours. This is because it could make your NFT irrelevant to buyers.

Once you own an NFT, the digital asset is yours to do with as you please. You can keep it as a collectible, display it for others to see, or use it as part of a larger digital project. You can also list it for sale. Marketplaces charge a fee for NFT sales. These fees can fluctuate based on the blockchain network the NFT uses since the blockchain computing needed to verify the NFT consumes energy, known as a "gas fee."

To sell a digital asset you own, the piece will need to be uploaded to your marketplace of choice, provided that marketplace supports the blockchain the NFT was built on. From there, you can choose to list it for sale at a set price or opt for an auction-style sale in which buyers place bids.

Once uploaded, the marketplace will verify the asset. After it's sold, the marketplace will handle the transfer of the NFT from the seller to the buyer and will also transfer crypto funds to your wallet less the listing fee and other related blockchain computing expenses.

WHAT ARE SIGNS OF A BAD NFT PROJECT

A bad NFT project will usually raise multiple red flags. These include but are not limited to too many mints, an excessive mint price, lack of liquidity, an anonymous founder team and lots of fake influencer accounts that are promoting the project's mint. Very often these projects will end in a so-called "rug pull", where the founding team disappears with all the money.

Now that we've established what sort of indicators will help you choose a big basket of prospects, let's have a closer look at the early warning signs of a scam or simply a bad project. Some of these red flags will be obvious to you and are easy to identify, while others are trickier.

In the end, it all depends on your personal risk appetite, but make sure you take note of these.

Too Many Mints

What makes a good NFT collection is not the number of mints you do.

If a project has already done a couple of mints and still hasn't gained notable traction, then it's definitely a red flag. This doesn't mean the team isn't trying, but it might mean they simply lack the ability to execute.

Since new mints indirectly dilute the value of the original collection, it simply doesn't add true value either. If the original collection doesn't sell, there is absolutely no reason to assume that it will work with the second or third mint.

Mint Price Is Too High

Over the past year, average mint prices have consistently increased. Part of that could be attributed to the high volatility of the ETH price.

But is that really what makes a good NFT project?

Considering that some of the most successful NFT projects of all time started with a free mint, asking for 0.5 ETH or more to mint new tokens seems a bit greedy.

That doesn't mean that a free mint will necessarily perform any better, but at least the burden of risk is shared between investors and founders.

Lack of Liquidity

Lack of price appreciation is one thing, lack of volume is another. A project can easily be undervalued if its trading volume is still relatively high.

Good trade volume also means that the project's treasury is filling up with funds to spend on growing the project. But if there's little trading volume, then it's also an increased risk for investors.

As an investor, you want to be sure that you can actually cash out of your position at a reasonable market price. If there's little demand, you may be forced to sell at a discount, even if the market price is already low.

In this case, the question of what makes a good NFT project becomes irrelevant because even if it was a good project, you still can't cash out.

Anonymous Team

We mentioned earlier that a doxxed team is a positive sign for a project. It's amongst what makes a good NFT project. And yes, an anonymous team is unfortunately a bad sign.

This does not mean that every anonymous founding team is automatically a scam or a rug pull. It also doesn't mean they can't turn it into a successful project.

However, the risk lies in the fact that anonymity reduces the founders' incentive to act in good faith. If you are anonymous, you have few consequences to fear if you mess up.

"Influencer" Accounts

If you see a new project being pumped on social media by a lot of Twitter accounts with thousands of followers (preferably with a stolen Bored Ape as their profile pic), then it might be a good idea to stay away.

You can identify these fake accounts by the constant giveaways that they organize. Some of them promise you NFT whitelist spots on a big upcoming project, though these can also be legitimate.

They usually promise people unrealistic amounts of free money or crypto for simply following them and liking their tweets. This is a huge red flag because it's a typical scam used to manipulate gullible people on the internet.

RISKS

The value of some NFTs has skyrocketed in the past year and attracted a lot of attention from the investment community. There certainly are some merits to consider when buying and using NFTs:

• Certain physical collectibles (such as art) have a long track record of appreciating in value, and digital art could exhibit the same price appreciation.

• Buying and selling digital assets as NFTs yields access to potentially far more buyers and sellers than in the past.

• Smart contracts can ensure that artists and creators get paid based on the use and resale of their work in the future.

But there are also some reasons not to invest in and use NFTs:

• Since most NFTs represent static assets that don't generate any income on their own, they are primarily valued by subjective metrics such as buyer demand. Consequently, sky-high prices may not last forever, and NFTs could lose considerable value.

• Creating and selling NFTs isn't free, and the fees can add up to more than an NFT is valued by other users on a marketplace.

- NFTs and the blockchain technology they're built on have an environmental impact since they use up a significant amount of energy to create and verify transactions.

THE FUTURE OF NFTS

Experts remain split on it. Some are screaming "bubble," while others claim NFTs will create new ownership opportunities, and remix old ones. Meanwhile, creators and artists are claiming this is the next form of monetization.

It's the technology behind the scenes of NFTs, the smart contracts on blockchain technology, that offers the real value.

Experts also say the NFT marketplace would need to become more accessible for everyday investors in order to be more widely adopted. OpenSea is the main peer-to-peer trading platform for NFTs, but there are other companies that want to bring NFTs more easily to the masses. Popular crypto exchange Coinbase, for example, recently announced plans to open a new marketplace where people can buy, sell and collect NFTs.

Printed in Great Britain
by Amazon

31643621R00030